trotman

REAL LIFE ISSUES:
BULLYING

Emma Caprez

Real Life Issues: Bullying
This first edition published in 2004 by Trotman and Company Ltd
2 The Green, Richmond, Surrey TW9 1PL

Reprinted 2005

© Trotman and Company Limited 2004

'Bully For You' reprinted by permission of PFD on behalf of
JOHN HEGLEY, © 2002 John Hegley

Editorial and Publishing Team
Author Emma Caprez
Editorial Mina Patria, Editorial Director; Rachel Lockhart, Commissioning Editor;
Anya Wilson, Managing Editor; Bianca Knights, Assistant Editor
Production Ken Ruskin, Head of Pre-press and Production;
James Rudge, Production Artworker
Sales and Marketing Deborah Jones, Head of Sales and Marketing
Advertising Tom Lee, Commercial Director
Managing Director Toby Trotman

Designed by XAB

British Library Cataloguing in Publication Data
A catalogue record for this book is available from the British Library

ISBN 0 85660 987 0

Typeset by Tradespools Publishing Solutions
Printed and bound in Great Britain by
Cromwell Press, Trowbridge, Wiltshire

CONTENTS:

'... getting bullied is NEVER YOUR FAULT, you are not a "victim". The problems lie with the people who choose to bully.'

REAL LIFE ISSUES:
Bullying

ABOUT THE AUTHOR

Emma Caprez studied for her BA (Hons) in Design and Media
Management at Thames Valley University. For her final-year project she
researched, wrote and illustrated a book on the history of the Ealing
School of Art and organised a follow-up exhibition and reunion. She
graduated with first class Honours in 1993. She has worked on several
research projects, including one on dramatherapy and the media, and
has contributed towards university literature. She has written for two
international music papers, *Rumba* and *LA Rock Review*, and has had
her photos published in *Melody Maker*. Emma has also written *Getting
into the Media* (and produced the video of the same name), *Getting
into Performing Arts*, *Journalism Uncovered*, *Art and Design
Uncovered* and *The Disabled Students' Guide to University*. Family
experience of bullying prompted Emma's concern in this area.

REAL LIFE ISSUES:
Bullying

ACKNOWLEDGEMENTS

This book is dedicated to Suky and J B and to all those children and young people who have experienced the anguish of bullying.

Huge thanks to Lynn Towers and Mandy Prowse for their additional research and help, and to all the contributors whose names have been changed for purposes of confidentiality.

Thanks also to: Pauline Hughes from ChildLine, Andrew Morrison from Kidscape; Moira Paterson from SMILE; Dunoon Grammar School in Scotland.

Massive thanks, love and happiness to my gorgeous Rook, Biba Maya, Suky Ella, all my family and the Bryer family too.

BULLY FOR YOU

If you're being bullied,
tell.
Tell your parents
tell your guardians
tell your carers,
tell your home-sharers
tell your teacher
tell your headteacher
tell your deputy headteacher
tell the teacher who is deputy headteacher
when the headteacher is away
and the deputy has to move up one, as well,
tell all of them.
TELL

John Hegley

FOREWORD

Have you ever heard any of these said about bullying?

- 'it's character-building'
- 'it's just a bit of fun'
- 'it's part of growing up'
- 'only victims get bullied.'

No. None of these things are true. It is certainly not character-building; it's quite the opposite, it's character-bashing. Bullying knocks your confidence and your self-esteem. If you're bullied you often feel there is something wrong with you and question your self-image and feelings of belonging to society. You can become withdrawn and shy and find it difficult to make friends. And as for fun, if it is fun, is *everyone* laughing? No, of course not. Part of growing up? Surely the best way to grow up is in an environment where positive social skills are fostered, not squashed by negative ones.

Children and young adults often become victims of bullying because of their differences (such as race, disability or sexuality), but only by people who are ignorant of these differences. Generally speaking there is no *particular* reason why someone is bullied: if someone wants to bully, they'll find any reason. Bullying affects your confidence and self-esteem, so that you might become an easier target, but getting bullied is NEVER YOUR FAULT, you are not a 'victim'. The problems lie with the people who choose to bully.

Remember, everyone deserves to be respected and feel safe. No one deserves to be bullied.

This book sets out to offer support to children and young people who are being bullied and to help those who bully to understand why they do it and find ways to put an end to it. I sincerely wish you a future free from bullying and full of the happiness you deserve. Best wishes.

INTRODUCTION

Courage is fire, and bullying is smoke.
Benjamin Disraeli (1804–81), novelist and twice Prime Minister

Bullying affects many children and young people throughout the UK every day. Bullying may be commonplace but it is completely unacceptable and should not be tolerated in any society. People should not have to live their lives in fear, with every day overshadowed by the overwhelming impact of bullying.

WHAT IS BULLYING?

Bullying is when a more dominant individual or group deliberately tries

FACT BOX

In June 2003, 74% of secondary school children and young people (aged 11–16) had seen a pupil verbally abused and 46% had seen a pupil kicked or hit.

Source: Department for Education and Skills (DfES)

to humiliate or upset a less dominant individual or group, causing physical pain and/or emotional distress. Bullying can take many different forms, from name-calling and exclusion to being forced to hand over your dinner money or being physically attacked. Bullying involves the abuse of power and can be a one-off incident or occur over a period of time.

The following two stories are from ChildLine, the free telephone helpline for children and young people. They demonstrate two different types of bullying.

Greg, 11, was terrified of going back to school on Mondays. 'This group of boys come and find me every playtime. They hit me, punch me, drag me around the playground and tear up my work. I'm always getting into trouble with the teachers for looking scruffy and not handing in my homework.' Greg told the counsellor that he had horrible nightmares every Sunday. 'I feel as if I can't ever get away from them – they wait for me after school. Last Friday I was hiding in the changing rooms and they found me and blocked the door. One of them had a knife.' The boys had threatened to 'batter him on Monday'.

Shamila, 15, called in tears saying that she dreaded going to school. She told her ChildLine counsellor how she used to be outgoing but she 'didn't like talking much now'. For the past month Shamila had been bullied by a gang of girls in her class because, she said: 'I'm about the only Asian girl in my school'. Shamila explained that she couldn't talk to her parents about how she was feeling because her mum and dad were not getting on very well and she didn't want to add to their worries.

Greg and Shamila got in touch with ChildLine to get guidance and advice on how to deal with their individual cases, and their problems are now sorted out. But what about you?

DOES BULLYING TAKE OVER YOUR LIFE?

Bullying can turn your life on its head and become the prime focus of your existence – your own private hell. It can lead to a number of consequences, from falling academic levels to serious psychiatric injury and even suicide.

But don't let things get this far. This book is here to help, by providing tips on how to prevent bullying and ways to deal with it.

HAVE YOU EVER BEEN BULLIED?

Most people have felt pushed around at some point in their lives, or been the butt of a joke they felt unhappy about. About half of all children will have experienced some bullying in their school lives and about a fifth will have endured a more serious level of bullying.

HAVE YOU EVER BEEN A BULLY?

Everyone is likely to indulge in a little bullying at one or another time in their life, but it's usually a one-off situation and we apologise afterwards. Bullying that is intended to cause distress, where there is no remorse and that occurs regularly is very serious.

Do you want to stop being a bully?

Being a bully may make you feel bad, guilty or really miserable. If you want to break the cycle of your bullying behaviour this book can help. Being a bully may not really be your chosen path, but you may feel it difficult to stop, especially if you are dominated by other bullies in a gang. Turning over a new leaf is not impossible. Acknowledging you have a problem with bullying is an important first step and this book will help encourage you to think about why you bully, and what you can do to stop.

WHAT THIS BOOK CAN DO FOR YOU

This book will look at possible strategies for prevention, how to change the way you respond to bullying, how to cope with bullying, and ways of breaking the cycle.

> **For a closer look at the effects of bullying on self-esteem, see *Real Life Issues: Confidence and Self-Esteem.***

CHAPTER ONE

ABOUT BULLYING
What does bullying mean?

'I was always being picked on because I couldn't read very well. We came to this country as refugees and I got bullied for that as well. I just tried really hard to be invisible so no one would notice me. I hated school and I hated myself for being so scared and not fitting in.'

Shiba, 19

HOW DO I KNOW IF I'M BEING BULLIED?

Bullying is intentional, not accidental, and is carried out in order to gain control over someone else. The bully doesn't apologise or try to make amends, which is what most of us would do if we didn't really intend to be mean. Shiba was being bullied by people who were both racist and ignorant and this made her unhappy about who she was.

Victims of bullying often blame themselves for being bullied, but no one deserves to be bullied. The bullies pick on people they see as an easy target – children or young people who are vulnerable (because they are younger, smaller, on their own, easy to scare and upset), not for any other reason.

Bullying can take a number of different forms:

- physical: kicking, hitting, pushing, shoving, punching, damaging your belongings, stealing your money
- verbal: abusive comments, threats and intimidation, name-calling, spreading rumours
- non-verbal: ignoring, turning away, excluding, rude gestures
- emotional/psychological: racist, sexist, homophobic comments, abuse about weight, height, disability, birthmarks, family, religion, etc.; mimicking you, e.g. if you stutter; treating you as inferior.

Other, newer, forms of bullying are delivering hate messages to mobile phones by text or voicemail, posting hurtful stories on websites and sending abusive emails.

WHAT IS TEASING?

'I was only teasing,' you hear people say, and that is meant to make you feel that it was all a joke and you obviously have no sense of humour.

Teasing is supposed to be OK. Everyone gets teased every now and then, and most of the time we don't mind. But when you analyse

FACT BOX

Four per cent of pupils in Year 8 reported that they had received nasty text messages and 2% had received nasty email messages.

Source: DfES

d be disguised as teasing, and if they were just teasing they
nudging you, winking at you and laughing together, but
hey are talking over you it is obvious they are deliberately
urt your feelings. You probably feel like saying something like
nse in (c), but this may encourage them to become more
robably the best thing to do is just ignore their comments,
u can't hear what they are saying and read a book. If you
enough you could get up and move to another seat, or
ff the bus and catch the next one.

in the playground and a girl comes up to you, starts
racist comments and then spits on you. Do you:

her and walk away?
er and spit back in her face?
, 'What makes you think I'm interested in what you have to
perfectly happy with the way I am.'
eel sorry for you, it must be really draining having so much
or something you don't understand'.

make racist comments are just ignorant. The best thing to
rtive and say something back; you will feel good about
or yourself. If you feel that she is liable to turn more
d that everything will just escalate, the best thing to do
walk away, but make sure you inform a member of staff.
erious offence and not to be tolerated in any school.

---

teasing (by saying the words plainly), the comments made are
generally a disguised way of trying to say something mean, and if we
respond in a negative way, the teaser acts as if we didn't get their joke.

'Whenever my uncle came to visit he would always try and put me
down. I think he was jealous of me for some reason – well, that's
what my mum said. He probably thought he was just teasing, but
he'd say stuff like I didn't know anything and he did. My mum said it
was because I knew more than he did and he didn't like it. I think he
was bullying me because of it.'

Sasha, 14

WHAT IS THE DIFFERENCE BETWEEN TEASING AND BULLYING?

If the teasing involves intimidation and if the person being teased ends
up feeling distressed, it is bullying. Where bullying is not intended the
person doing the teasing will immediately apologise and say that they
hadn't meant to hurt you.

Is there a difference between being bullied and being used as a
scapegoat? (A scapegoat is someone who is used as a target for
blame and responsibility. The scapegoat is discredited while the
perpetrator gets away with it.) Being used as a scapegoat can be a
form of bullying if a person (or group of people) is abusing their
power by putting blame on to someone less able to stand up for
themselves. It can be very distressing and damaging to the scapegoat's
confidence and self-esteem to be treated as though you are in the
wrong when you are not.

IS PHYSICAL BULLYING WORSE THAN OTHER FORMS OF BULLYING?

Non-physical bullying is harder to recognise but can be just as destructive as physical bullying. You've heard of the theory that 'Sticks and stones may break my bones, but words can never hurt me'? I think the person who first said this was trying hard to convince him or herself that abusive comments and nasty rumours don't really touch you, but we all know that words are immensely powerful, and when people are derogatory or disrespectful to you it can be earth-shattering and really destroy your self-image, self-esteem and confidence. So don't feel that you are being petty if you get upset by non-physical forms of bullying. Everyone deserves to be treated with respect.

Does television encourage respect?

Television programmes like *Weakest Link* and *Hell's Kitchen* tend to glamorise bullying and make it seem acceptable behaviour. The viewers are almost like bystanders who witness an act of bullying but do nothing about it. These programmes may just be a gimmick, and the contestants willing victims, but is it sending out the right message to children and young people about ways to behave? They certainly don't seem to reinforce consideration, empathy and respect.

THE DIFFERENCE BETWEEN BOYS AND GIRLS

'When I got bullied by these boys that lived up the road from me there was no way I could tell my old man. I knew he'd tell me that I had to stand up to them and be macho and stuff, but I couldn't.'

Alex, 14

Historically, boys have been more conne[c]
punching, kicking, etc., and girls with verb[al]
rumours and name-calling. However, ther[e]
the incidence of girls being violent, which
increase may be for many reasons: ther[e]
models in the media; more women ind[
there's a belief that being aggressive giv[
being assertive is sometimes confused

WHERE DOES [IT] HAPPEN?

We tend to think of bullying as someth[ing]
places where there is little, if any, adu[lt]
playground, the corridors and the toile[t]
sorts of environments, for example:

- on the way to and from school
- in the park or playground
- at home
- at work
- in prisons and detention centres

> **1** You are sitting on the school [bus]
> the year above come and sit [
> you as though you weren't th[ere]
> Someone's got serious BO r[
> windows.' What do you do?
>
> **a** Ignore their comments and [
> **b** Say, 'excuse me,' and move [
> bus driver.
> **c** Say, 'Yeah, I can smell that [

This cou[
would be [
because [
trying to [
the respo[
abusive. [
pretend y[
feel stron[
even get [

2 You're [
makin[

a Ignore [
b Insult [
c Tell he[
say? I'[
d Say, 'I [
hatred

People who [
do is be ass[
standing up [
aggressive a[
would be to [
Racism is a s[

CHAPTER TWO:

WHY DO PEOPLE BULLY?
Some causes of bullying

Many studies show that children who continue to bully past a certain age end up having problems as adults. A study conducted by Dan Olweus in Norway concluded that children who are bullies at the age of eight are four times as likely to end up in prison than non-bullies. These findings have been reflected in other studies. Other outcomes include: problems forming lasting relationships; alcohol or drug dependency; a continuation of aggressive and anti-social behaviour; and a higher risk of unemployment. So it is very important that if you do bully you seek help to stop.

FACT BOX

Nine out of ten people in two young offenders' institutes who were interviewed by Kidscape were involved in bullying while at school.

Source: Kidscape

WHAT SORT OF PEOPLE BULLY?

Anyone can be a bully, including:

- schoolchildren
- siblings
- parents
- step-parents/step-siblings
- other relations
- teachers
- girlfriends/boyfriends.

It is not just schoolchildren or young people who bully. Adults may take advantage of their power to humiliate you in front of other people. Sometimes this act of belittling is done to make them feel more important or higher in the family hierarchy or relationship. Adults bully children by shouting and aggression and teasing or making fun of you. This isn't to say that every time a parent or sibling screams he or she is a bully. Most people raise their voice from time to time when things get difficult at home, but they are not intending to hurt you. But continually using physical aggression (punching, kicking) or derogatory put-downs ('You're such a fat pig – you'll never get a boyfriend, no one will want you') when you've done nothing to deserve it is not acceptable behaviour. Girlfriends or boyfriends may also bully in order to control their relationship with you, to ensure the relationship is on their terms, with your needs being very insignificant.

BULLYING INDIVIDUALLY AND IN GANGS

Bullies can operate alone and, more commonly, in gangs. The ringleader will recruit other people to be in his or her gang, generally by means of intimidation, such as, 'If you join my gang, you'll be all right,' or in other words, 'you won't get bullied'.

CHLOE'S STORY

'I was really scared of this girl at our school. She used to pick on everybody and she was always threatening to start fights. She told me that she wouldn't give me any grief if I joined her gang and I was so scared of her I agreed. Then I ended up backing her up when she was being mean and laughing at the nasty things she said, even if I didn't find them funny. Part of me felt it was wrong, but the other half enjoyed the way people would do anything we said.' **Chloe, 14**

WHY DO PEOPLE BULLY?

If you're a kind, considerate person, it may be incomprehensible to you that anyone would choose deliberately to distress another person, but there are lots of reasons why people bully. These include:

- anger
- jealousy
- insecurity
- self-loathing
- unhappiness
- unworthiness
- low self-esteem
- to fit in
- enjoying the feeling of power
- being spoilt
- to show off and look tough
- to avoid being bullied
- to get attention
- family problems
- they are being used as a scapegoat or being bullied themselves

- they are under pressure to succeed
- they feel friendless and lonely
- prejudices, e.g. racial or homophobic prejudices.

MASON'S STORY

'My mum got married to this new bloke and I didn't like him. He was always shouting and telling me what to do and stuff. It used to really annoy me 'cause he wasn't my dad. Then I started getting into trouble at school because of my behaviour. I was picking on this boy in our class because he was always putting his hand up to answer the questions and stuff and I made him give me his dinner money.'

Mason, 15

People who are bullies often have their own problems: maybe an inability to control their anger, violence at home, parents divorcing, feeling unloved or not liking themselves. They might feel they need to bully in order to make people fear them so that they can feel important.

People who bully often have poor social skills and find it hard to make friends. Bullying helps them achieve a certain level of popularity and status. They may also find it difficult to express their emotions, maybe because they feel – or have been taught – that it is a sign of weakness to do so. In fact, it's a sign of strength to be able to express yourself. Children who bully may come from homes where family members do not feel much warmth or affection towards one another. They may come from families where there is little structure or monitoring of behaviour, or from homes that are very regimented and where physical punishment is used.

WHAT DO BULLIES HOPE TO ACHIEVE?

The reason people bully is to bring about a negative response, such as fear, humiliation, anger and upset.

For the bullied this means:
- fear
- tears
- upset
- humiliation
- anger
- anxiousness
- helplessness
- feeling that there is something wrong with you
- feeling unsafe
- loneliness and isolation
- feeling that no one likes you.

For the bully this means:
- feeling better/more powerful
- boosting low self-esteem
- fitting in
- getting attention
- getting respect
- being revered/feared.

1 *You have just left school when a gang of boys from another school corner you and ask you to hand over your mobile phone. You notice that one of the boys has a flick-knife in his hand. He isn't actually pointing it at you ... yet. What do you do?*

a Hand over the phone, of course. Your safety is more important than a phone, which can be replaced.

b There's no way you're going to hand over the phone – it was a birthday present. Just say, 'No way'.

c Beg them not to take your phone, you've only just got it and your dad will go mad if you come home without it.

Hand the phone over and get away from them as soon as possible. If they have a knife you don't know what could happen to you if you refuse them. There is no point in begging – boys like this won't be the slightest bit interested in what will happen to you if you go home without your phone, but they will probably really enjoy watching you squirm. If you beg it will just make them feel even more powerful. Being in possession of an offensive weapon is also very serious and your parents or caregiver should report this incident to the police.

2 *There's this boy who sits on your table at school. He is a well-known bully and you're pretty scared of him. He tells you to join his gang or else. What do you do?*

a Join his gang, of course, you don't want to be on the wrong side of him.

b Say you don't want to very firmly, because you know even if you do, he's bound to turn on you and bully you at some point anyway. Then go and tell a member of staff or trusted adult what has happened.

c Say you're a bit busy with things at the moment, so you don't know if you'll be able to fit the gang in right now, but maybe some other time.

d Say, no, I don't want to – if you want to hang out as friends sometime, that might be possible, but not if any bullying is going to take place.

Options b and d would be the best response. He might actually admire you for standing up to him – sometimes what bullies really want is someone to say no to them. He might also be really chuffed that you would consider being a friend, which might be all he's really after, but just doesn't know how to go about it. Definitely don't agree to join in – giving a flimsy excuse won't get you anywhere. He'll realise you're so scared you'll be easy to recruit.

CHAPTER THREE:

HOW TO TACKLE BULLYING
Some strategies

SAVANNAH'S STORY

'It happened when I first started school in reception and lasted till Year 3. One of my classmates wanted me to just play with her and no one else. She was an only child and seemed to get whatever she wanted and needed a best buddy, probably because she had so many childminders as both her mum and dad worked. She was OK in class but really mean in the playground. This made me scared and I dreaded playtimes. I had to play with her or she would tell her mum or teacher and I was scared of going to the Head.

'I became cross because she wouldn't let me do anything I wanted to do and I started to feel scared about going to school. I ended up having tantrums at home, but my mum and dad talked a lot with me and we sorted it out. They took me to the Head and we talked with my teacher, but they said they couldn't really do anything as it was just her character and to just ignore her and play as a group. She left in Year 3 because her mother wanted a better school for her. We did make up before she left. She also started to get bullied and I wanted to stand up for her. It has taught me to understand my friends better

and try and find out why they do the things they do. I now stand up
for myself a bit more and walk away.' **Savannah, 12**

ChildLine believes that children are increasingly getting the message
that they should not have to put up with bullying and that they have a
right to be helped.

This chapter concentrates on strategies to avoid bullying and how to
deal with bullying if it happens. Not all suggestions will work for all
cases, and you might need to try a number of tactics to find the right
solution for you.

WAYS TO AVOID BULLYING

Prevention is better than cure, so try to avoid any potential bullying:
and if you are being bullied, try to avoid further bullying. The following
tips might be useful:

- avoid people who you know are bullies
- avoid places where bullying normally takes place
- keep near other children or staff
- don't bring valuable items or lots of money into school
- when you're on the bus, sit near the bus driver or other adults
- look confident (even if you don't feel it) and walk tall
- practise being assertive
- be accepting and confident about your differences.

If you stay away from the bullies, they are less able to bully you. If
possible, don't sit near them in class, avoid areas that are not closely
monitored by staff and don't use alleyways as shortcuts if you know
bullies hang out there.

When bullies are about, make sure you keep close to other friends – there is strength in numbers. If you don't have any friends to play with, make sure you keep near to a group of other children or playground staff. Alternatively, go to the library or lunchtime clubs, if these are available, and try to make some friends.

Never bring to school valuable items or things that you are particularly attached to. This will just make you a target for the bullies. If you do get caught and they ask you to hand over your money, you won't be able to if you haven't got any on you.

Bullies are basically cowards, which is why they mostly pick on vulnerable people. If you sit near the driver or other adults on the bus they are less likely to come and bother you, and if they do then you will have adult witnesses who will probably intervene. You could also try to vary your routes home so that the bullies won't know where to find you, or walk with other people so you are less vulnerable. You could also try to leave school earlier if possible, or later, when the bullies will no longer be around.

EMMA'S STORY

'I used to live quite a way from my school and I had to take two buses to get there. As I was the only person on the first bus from my school, I made an easy target for this bunch of girls from another school. They used to call me "slag" and things like that and I used to say, "yes, that's right", and just agree with what they'd said. That really confused them. One day my friend was coming to my house and we were sitting upstairs on the bus. They started throwing lit matches at us. We said nothing, just got up and went downstairs and sat by the driver. I always sat downstairs after that and they never bothered me again.' **Emma, 18**

If you lack confidence, it will show in the way you carry yourself. Body language is so important. It sends out messages to other people about the way you are feeling. If you are being bullied, the chances are your confidence and self-esteem will be severely affected and your body language will reflect this, making you even more vulnerable to being picked on by bullies. Think about your posture and try this exercise.

Walk with your back slouched, head down and your shoulders drooping forward. How does this make you feel? Now compare that feeling to walking with your back straight, head up and shoulders down. Look in the mirror at these two postures and ask yourself, do I come across as more confident when I am walking in a more confident manner?

BEING ASSERTIVE

There are basically three ways in which we can respond to other people:

- passively
- aggressively
- assertively.

When we respond **passively** to someone, we view the other person or people as being more important than us. For example: a boy in your class tells you to carry his bags home from school because he doesn't want to carry them himself. A passive person would agree to this request.

People who are passive tend to be pushed around and are often called doormats. It doesn't mean that you enjoy being a doormat: you're just not assertive enough to stand up for yourself and your rights, so you put up with being used instead.

When we respond **aggressively** to someone, we tend to view the other person as being less important than us, or have less respect for them. For example: your mother asks you to lay the table for dinner and you reply, 'No, why the hell should I? You're the mother round here, that's your job. I'm watching TV.' This behaviour makes the other person feel uncomfortable and hurt.

Assertive people view the other person as *equally* important as themselves. Being assertive means saying what you want, firmly, without disrespecting the other person.

Kidscape have outlined the basic reasons for being assertive. Every individual possesses these human rights:
- to be treated with respect
- to make mistakes and be responsible for them
- to refuse requests without having to feel guilty or selfish
- to ask for what you want (realising the other person has the right to say 'no')
- to be listened to and be taken seriously
- to say, 'I don't understand'
- to ask for information.

Assertiveness exercises

In the following exercise you can practise with a friend or relation, or just talk to yourself in the mirror. Practise asking for something directly, politely, concisely and firmly. Look at the person, or your reflection, in the eye, so that you can show you are confident about what you are saying.
- don't do that, please, I don't like it
- that's my packet of crisps, can you give it back, please?
- my jacket suits you, but I want it back now, please

- I didn't understand the homework, please could you explain it to me?
- I'm sorry but I can't help you with your school project because I have a lot of work to do myself.

Think about situations in which you haven't been able to stand up for yourself, or when you have ended up pushing someone around. Practise saying what you should have said, so that if the situation arises again you will be able to deal with it in a more assertive manner.

If you have been asked to do something that you don't want to do, and have said no, but are being repeatedly pestered about it, make sure you stick to your original answer and refuse to be swayed, even if this means having to say no, No, NO, **NO**, *NO!* lots of times until they give up. Make sure you look the person in the eye and stand confidently so that they know you are not going to back down. It may be that you could offer to do something else as an alternative or compromise, but it must be something you are happy about doing.

CELEBRATING DIFFERENCE

If you feel you are different in some way – maybe you're a wheelchair user, taller than all the other kids in your class, gay, have a birth mark, the only Asian girl at school, your mother has a mohican and wears a nosechain, or you dress differently from everyone else – make sure you celebrate it. It's wonderful to be different and if you feel confident about your differences, you won't be affected by abusive comments from people who are ignorant about them. Be proud of yourself.

It is sometimes a good idea to get involved in groups with other children or young people who have the same 'difference' as you. For example, if you stutter you may find that being with or talking to other people who stutter will make you feel less isolated and more accepting.

'The other day, the bullies started having a go at me about my hair. I just said, "I like to be different and you've all got short hair, so I thought I'd have mine long." They didn't have anything to say after that.'

Simon, 11

Your uncle comes round to your house, and he is always trying to wind you up. He says, 'What have you got on? You look like a dyke/nancy boy'. Do you:

a Say, 'Oh shut up! You really get on my nerves. I wish you'd go away!' and storm out of the room, slamming the door.

b Say, 'Oh, sorry, I'll go and get changed then,' and go and find something else to wear.

c Say, 'Well I like it, so it's a good job I don't have to rely on your opinion about what to wear.'

Your uncle has verbally abused you and he is being homophobic, neither of which is acceptable. The best thing you can do is not to show your upset at what he has said, because that's what he's after. Option (c) is the best response because you have made it clear that you're happy with the way you look and you really don't give a hoot what he thinks.

HOW TO DEAL WITH BULLYING AS IT HAPPENS

Arming yourself with lots of tactics to help stop bullying can only be a positive thing. Here are some tips on what to do or say if you are being bullied.

Saying no

Simply saying no, assertively and perhaps loudly (to attract attention from a nearby teacher or a bystander who may go and get help), may be enough to deter a bully. If they realise you're not going to put up with their behaviour they might just give up.

Asking why

Sometimes it may be a good idea to ask why s/he is being mean to you. Just saying these words out loud for the bully to hear might make them realise that what they are doing is really unacceptable and may make them think about whether or not they want to continue to be mean.

Ignoring

Ignoring is a good way of making the bully realise that you're not interested in what they have to say. When I was at school, if I got repeated verbal abuse, I would give a slightly exaggerated yawn – not an overly sarcastic one and not aimed directly at them, as this would defeat the point of ignoring them. The yawn would just show them in a shorthand way that I found it pathetic that they couldn't think of anything better to say, and that the fact that they were repeating it yet again was extremely dull. I also have to add that I was never threatened with physical bullying as a consequence of my actions, otherwise I don't think I would have provoked them with a yawn.

Walking or running away

This is nothing to be ashamed of. If someone is bullying you, why should you stand there and just take it? Walking away shows you are simply not interested in what they have to say, and if you run away, it means you're clever enough not to hang around to be hurt. If you're cornered this may not be possible, in which case you could perhaps try the trick of pretending that someone is coming and when they turn away, run!

Hiding your emotions

The bully is always trying to provoke a negative emotion in you. Bullies want to see you upset, hurt or humiliated. The best way you can prevent them from achieving their goal is by hiding the way you are truly feeling and not show any of the desired responses. Look indifferent, laugh with them (even if the idea is that they should be laughing *at* you) or just have no expression at all.

Fogging

Fogging means either agreeing with what they are saying or giving an ambiguous answer, which could mean you're agreeing and disagreeing at the same time. This is a great way of brushing off the offensive abuse that a bully might like to throw at you. It's all about refusing to respond in a way that the bully wants you to. It puts you in control of the situation, and generally makes the bully feel either confused, disappointed not to have upset you, or irritated that you have made him/her look pathetic.

For example, the bully says, 'You are such a geek!' and you reply, possibly with a broad smile:

- 'Do you know, I think you're right. I am a geek. Thanks for that'
- 'Yes, I know'

■ 'Do you really think so? I was wondering that myself'

■ 'I know, it's great!'

'I remember when I was at primary school, kids used to say to me, "You get all your clothes from Oxfam," and I used to reply, "Yes, that's right", even though I didn't, just so they wouldn't have the reaction they wanted. They soon gave up after that.'

Emma, 18

Witty retorts

Thinking up something funny to say in response to bullying can be very effective, especially if it makes the bully look small, but beware of saying anything that could make him or her really angry and start being more aggressive towards you.

For example: 'You are so uncool. You're wearing Shell Dust trainers. Don't you know how old-fashioned they are? You should be wearing Bobby Jumps. You're such a loser.' You could reply, 'I like to be different. I guess that separates us lions from you sheep.'

Changing phone numbers and email addresses

If you've been receiving malicious phone calls, texts or emails, you could change your phone number and/or email address. Make sure you only hand out your new number and address to those people you absolutely trust, and ask them not to pass it on to anyone else unless they check with you first. If you've received an abusive email, keep a copy of it and show it to someone you trust; it's possible that the sender has committed a criminal offence. For more information on cyberstalking, check out the Bullying Online website, details in the Directory.

If you receive offensive or threatening phone messages they can be traced whether they're from a private, public or mobile phone. Harassment is a criminal offence and if it continues the police will take action.

CONTACT LISTS

It is always useful to have a card on you that lists the people you trust and who you might need to contact in case of an emergency or if you are bullied. If you have thought about who you might like to contact ahead of time, you will have their number or email address at hand. The quicker you deal with a situation, the quicker you nip it in the bud.

YOUR SAFETY COMES FIRST

There are some situations that are impossible to deal with on your own, for example if you're being attacked by a gang of bullies or if the bully is carrying an offensive weapon. Your safety is the most important concern and it is not a good idea to risk getting badly hurt. The most important thing is to get away safely, even if that means having to hand over your mobile phone or money. Possessions are never as important as you are. As soon as you've got away, go and tell an adult and you can take it from there.

WHAT TO DO WHEN YOU'VE BEEN BULLIED

SOPHIE'S STORY

'One day at school, this boy took my drink off me, and so I got it back off him. I think he didn't like it that I was a girl and was strong enough to do that. Anyway, I went off and was looking through the

window of this other class and he came right up behind me and punched me in the head. He pushed my head against the wall and then punched and kicked me in the back. I got a really bad headache. Someone told the teacher, but all that happened was that this boy, Lucas, got told off. When I told my mum, she came into the school and spoke to my teacher and said she didn't feel that just telling him off was enough. This boy was always hitting and kicking people – generally without any provocation. Eventually my mum spoke to the deputy head and steps were taken to sort it out. Things got better, but then I started an afterschool football club which was a mixed team. He started picking on me there too, calling me "arsehole" and swearing at me and stuff, and kicking and punching me. I did go back to the club a couple of times and my mum complained again. The deputy headteacher came and watched the match without Lucas knowing to sort out the problem, but I left the club anyway.'
Sophie, 13

It's good to talk

The first thing to do is find someone you trust that you can talk to. This could be a:

- teacher
- parent
- best friend
- family friend or relation
- doctor
- ChildLine (or other) counsellor.

Sometimes it feels risky to tell someone that you are being bullied, but not confiding in someone is generally worse. If you don't speak out it is likely that the bullying will escalate. Although talking is scary, doing nothing and hoping the bullying will just stop is usually not the answer.

Sometimes just being able to tell someone what has been going on, listen to their advice and discuss possible options will be of tremendous support.

TEACHERS

Teachers have a legal obligation to make sure that their pupils are safe at school, so they should do their utmost to sort out the problem. It is good if you can talk to a teacher as soon as the bullying has happened so that the situation can be dealt with straightaway. If you feel that your teacher won't take the incident seriously, then find another member of staff at school to speak to, perhaps a teacher you get on well with or the school nurse. Your school may have a teacher or school counsellor with specific anti-bullying responsibilities.

If you're concerned that talking to the teacher will make the bullying worse, ask to speak to them in confidence. This means you can say what you want and name the people involved, but they must not do anything that you haven't agreed to (e.g. reveal your name). You might not want them to pass on what you've said to anyone else. What is the school's anti-bullying policy? (See Chapter 4 for more details.)

HARRIET'S STORY

'Back in Year 9, when I was 15, I started a modelling career. A number of students in my class didn't think I was good enough and thought I was big-headed, so started to make nasty comments behind my back. The more modelling work I got the more they attacked me and started to threaten to beat me up. I started to feel scared and intimidated, not wanting to go to school. I didn't tell anyone at home, I wanted to try and deal with it myself, but then it started to get out of hand. One day after school I was going to brush my teeth ready for a casting and they cornered me. The leader

*pushed my toothbrush down my throat. I finally decided to pluck up
the courage and talk to my art teacher who I got on really well with
and trusted. She waited outside school for me for a couple of weeks.*

*'The first week they got worse, teasing me for telling a teacher and
being a chicken. My art teacher told me to try and ignore them, which
I did and they got bored. She told me to go straight to her if I needed
her again as dealing with it straight away nips it in the bud. I'd had
problems before with a couple of friends, but it had ended badly, but
this time it got sorted out. These incidents have caused me to be
mistrusting of people and I don't build many close friendships. What it
taught me is to try and walk away, ignore things that are hurtful and
don't let people see you upset. I have had occasions since where very
dominating people have tried to bully me or destroy my confidence,
but I think I am now able to brush them off and not get sucked in by
others' lack of confidence.'* **Harriet, 19**

Harriet's life was made hell by girls who were jealous of her success as a
model, but confiding in a teacher helped to end this episode of bullying.

PARENTS/CAREGIVERS

Talking to your parent or caregiver can be a huge relief. As well as
offering you advice and speaking to your teacher, they can also
provide emotional support.

You may worry that your parents might get upset, angry or both. They
probably will, but if you discuss the issue in the security of your own
home you can tell them how important it is that this issue be handled
sensitively. Your parents can be an enormous help. Ask them to
contact some of the organisations listed in the Directory for further
help and guidance.

You may also be concerned that your parents will think you're being a wimp and should be able to sort the bullies out. This is more likely to be the case if you're male. Tell them that hitting back can sometimes make the situation worse: you don't want to end up being accused of being a bully and getting into trouble at school.

You may also worry that your parents will not believe you. The only way you can find out is by telling them. If they refuse to believe you no matter what you say, then turn to one of the other people listed above for support. Don't give up. Just because your parents don't believe you doesn't mean everyone else will think you're making it up.

Finally, you may not be able to talk to your parent/s because it is your mum and/or dad who is bullying you. In this case, turn to someone who you can trust and let them know what's going on. Together you can seek help.

FRIENDS
A close and trustworthy friend is always a good person to confide in. They might know the bully/ies and might have some suggestions on how to tackle the problem – it could be something as simple as making sure you keep together – or they can go with you for moral support when you tell your teacher or parent.

DOCTORS
It can help to talk to your doctor. You may not classify yourself as ill, but the psychological and/or physical effects of being bullied can cause great stress, and your doctor can help with this. He or she may be able to write a letter to your school about the effect that the bullying is having on your health.

COUNSELLORS

If you can't think of anyone you would feel safe talking to, then try one of the helplines listed in the Directory, such as ChildLine. ChildLine is a free helpline for children and young adults and it is completely confidential. You will talk to a fully trained counsellor who will have experience of counselling children who have been bullied and will know what steps you, your family and school can take to stop it. This service is completely confidential, so no one will know that you've made the call or what you've said. The call doesn't even show up on your phone bill, although if you call from a mobile or cable phone it might. ChildLine is used by many children so sometimes the lines are busy, but don't give up. Keep trying and you will get through, or try one of the other helplines in the meantime.

Kirsty, aged nine, wrote to ChildLine because she was being bullied at school. 'As soon as I get to school it starts. They throw my school books around and call me names. The second our teacher goes out of the class it starts again.' Kirsty said she was ashamed to tell anyone how she was feeling and wanted ChildLine to tell her how she could stop this happening to her.

Eight-year-old Billy told his ChildLine counsellor: 'I can't go to school, I just can't.' He had just jumped off the school bus to call ChildLine. Other children on the bus had been teasing him – snatching his school bag, throwing things at him, thumping him on the head and in the chest and calling him names.

Some children and young people find it easier to talk to someone who doesn't know them. Four times as many girls contact ChildLine as boys, so ChildLine have launched a campaign called Boys Allowed: this aims to encourage boys and young men to understand that asking for help and advice is a sign of strength, not weakness. If you are wondering whether to call ChildLine, have a look at their website for more information.

Helplines or chatlines you can contact include:
- ChildLine
- Kidscape
- Anti-bullying Network
- NSPCC
- Samaritans
- Bullying Online.

FACT BOX

Some facts and figures:
- *Bullying is the single most common reason why children phone ChildLine*
- *During the year from 1 April 2002 to 31 March 2003, ChildLine received more than 20,000 calls about bullying*
- *More 12-year-olds call ChildLine about bullying than any other age group*
- *ChildLine believes that children are increasingly getting the message that they should not have to put up with bullying and that they have a right to be helped.*

Source: ChildLine

You can rehearse what it is you want to say, or even write it down if you feel it would be difficult to talk. Another useful tip is to keep a record of everything that has gone on and how it has made you feel – almost like a diary. This can also help if you talk to your parents.

It is important that the person you choose to talk to understands that it is up to you how the problem is dealt with. For example, you might want your parents to report the problem to the school only on condition that your name is not mentioned when the bullies are dealt with (chances are, you're not the only person they are bullying); or that the bullies' names are not mentioned, but the school is told in general terms that there is a problem.

Write a letter

If you simply cannot bring yourself to talk, write down a full account of what has been happening to you and the distress you are feeling in a letter and give, post or email it to someone you trust.

Document when bullying occurs

This is useful because you may not remember all the details and there may be a time when you will need to show this record as evidence of what has gone on, for example if you are applying to transfer to another school where places are limited.

- Writing is a way of releasing your feelings, especially if you find it hard to talk
- Keeping a diary means that you will have a record of what has occurred and a list of who was involved. Mention whether there were any bystanders who would be able to verify what you have said
- If you are physically injured, take photographs of your cuts and bruises.

Get support

If you know of other children at school who are being bullied, approach them and make friends. You may be able to deal with the problem collectively, which is much easier than dealing with it alone.

Changing schools

'I hated my old school, because from the moment I stepped through the door I was picked on for being Asian. I was called racist names and accused of smelling. It was hell. In the end I started refusing to go to school and my mum then decided I should try going to another school. My new school is further away but has more Asian kids in it and I feel much more comfortable. I still find it hard to make friends, but it's much better here.'

Komal, 14

You may feel that the only way to avoid further bullying is to change schools. Research has found a number of criteria that schools low in bullying share. These criteria are worth looking at with your parents or caregiver before making the move:

- Is the school honest? Schools that say bullying does not exist may not be confronting or acknowledging the problem
- Is high priority given to sorting out the problems of bullying?
- Does the school have open communication? Are children encouraged to talk when they or their friends are experiencing problems?
- Does the school involve teachers, pupils and parents in making decisions on how to tackle bullying?
- Is the school small?
- Are the class sizes small?
- Are the classes across age ranges?
- Is there less deprivation in the area?

■ Is the ethos of the school to foster a caring, less competitive environment?

Some of these factors, such as small class sizes and cross-age-range classes, will be difficult to find in a state school. Even if you were able to find a school that met all these criteria, it wouldn't necessarily mean that bullying doesn't exist – but it may mean that it is harder for it to do so.

Home education

Another alternative to school is to be educated at home. A lot of children who have been bullied have found this a successful move. This is obviously not an option for everyone and you will need the full support of your parents or caregiver. Further information about being educated at home can be found in the Directory.

Courses

Kidscape runs one-day ZAP courses, which help children and young people to feel better about themselves and become more assertive. It's also a chance to meet with other children and young people who have experienced bullying.

---

1 You are in the playground. Three kids from the year above come over, take your hat off your head and start throwing it to each other. Do you:

a Say nothing – it's not worth the aggravation – but just feel really cross inside.

b Shout, 'Give that back, you pathetic losers', and kick one of them in the leg.

c Say firmly, 'Hey, that's my hat and I want it back. Give it back now.'

Sometimes kids think this kind of behaviour is funny, but if you are clearly upset about it, then they have overstepped the mark and are probably just trying to have fun at your expense. Saying nothing is like allowing them to get away with it, but if they are known bullies and are likely to get aggressive, it may be best to say nothing and hope they give it back, or report it to a teacher. Shouting abuse at them and kicking is not going to help anyone – they may hit you back harder. The best option is to say firmly that you want it back. If they don't return it then go and speak to a teacher or get your friends to help you get the hat back.

2 You are hanging out with a group of kids at the local park and one of them gets out a joint. He passes it round, and everyone has a smoke. Then they pass it to you. You don't want to have any, but you know they'll have a go at you if you refuse. What do you do?

a Take the joint and have a smoke. You don't want to deal with the consequences of saying no.

b Say, 'Oh, I can't smoke at the moment, I had a really bad asthma attack the other day', and hope they'll leave you alone.

c Say, 'No thanks', firmly, and if they ask again say, 'No, I don't want to, thanks, I'm not into it', and stand your ground.

Good friends would never force you to do something you don't want to. If they give you a hard time about your decision then you should find yourself some other friends who won't try and push you around. There may be other young people in the group who would like to say no – if you say no, they might feel stronger about refusing as well. If they are persistent you could ask them why they feel it is so important for you to be involved. Are they scared of doing it without you?

CHAPTER FOUR:

WHAT CAN BE DONE TO STOP BULLYING?
Schools, pupils, friends

WHAT SCHOOLS CAN DO

In 1998 the School Standards and Framework Act came into force. This stated that every school is responsible for initiating its own anti-bullying strategy.

The School Standards and Framework Act states that headteachers must outline measures, including rules (and methods of enforcing

'... some teachers were identified as better at dealing with bullying than others. Such teachers were reported to be better at listening to pupils, more prepared to take them seriously, and to take "firm but fair" action.'

Source: *Tackling Bullying: listening to the views of children and young people*, DfES

these rules), in order to ensure good behaviour by pupils, respect for each other and prevention of all forms of bullying. This Act applies in England and Wales only, but government ministers and school inspectors in Scotland issue similar advice to deal with the problem of bullying. So schools have a legal responsibility to keep their pupils safe.

SIMON'S STORY

'I had been previously bullied, but then this new boy started at our school. He wasn't too bad in Year 3, but things got worse when I went into Year 4 and is still going on now I'm in Year 5. This new boy is really fit and buff and likes to show off. He has other kids in his gang now too. It started off with them saying stuff about my hair, then my clothes and basically a lot of teasing and saying mean things. Then they started doing things like cornering me. There's three of them in particular and they surround me so that I am pushed up against the wall. They hit and kick me and stuff like that. One day I was off school so my friend James got picked on. I found out that they picked on him because I wasn't there to have a go at. They also do things like hide my lunch box so I can't eat. My mum just thought I was too busy playing football to want to eat my lunch. They have also hid my PE kit a few times too, which meant I ended up getting into trouble with the teacher, because I told her I forgot it.

'These bullies have told me that if I join their gang they'll stop bullying me. I have always said no, but another friend of mine joined their gang, and when he turned to start picking on me as well, I just said, "How can you do this? You know what it feels like," and he stopped doing it.

'My parents ended up finding out and telling the headteacher, even though I didn't want them to. My mum told the headteacher not to *mention my name, but my class teacher did and then I had all of them calling me a snitch. I don't trust any of the teachers now.*

'I often feel completely sick before I have to go to school, and it doesn't go away till I get home. But I have learnt a few things recently about how to react when they say mean things – like pretending I haven't heard them and not showing them I'm upset – and it does seem to work.' **Simon, 11**

Of course, not all teachers are as insensitive as Simon's, and there are a lot of positive steps schools can take, such as:

- Conduct a whole-school survey to find out about the extent of bullying in the school, where the hotspots (places where bullying is more likely to occur) are, and what type of bullying is going on
- Monitor hotspots such as toilets, the school entrance, corridors, in classes before the teacher arrives, certain areas of the playground, etc.
- Get each class to come up with ideas for rules about behaviour. The pupils and teachers then draw up a contract, sign it and pin it up in the class for all to see
- Encourage regular assemblies, class discussions, projects, etc. on defining what bullying and good social skills are. These should be continual, not one-offs
- Invite outside organisations, such as ChildLine and Kidscape, to do some training with the pupils, teachers and other school staff
- Ensure that incidents of bullying are taken seriously and dealt with, and that positive social skills are taught
- Make sure that pupils are positioned in class so that people who have been bullied are not sitting near to bullies and bullies are sitting near to the teacher and in full view (not with their backs to them)

- Set up support schemes that encourage positive friendships, such as lunchtime activity-focused clubs
- Set up peer support schemes
- Encourage children to try and prevent, support and stop children being bullied
- Make confidential sources of advice and support available both within school and in partnership with relevant organisations outside school
- Encourage a whole-school policy of speaking out
- Take seriously all incidents reported to staff by pupils
- Support pupils' rights to confidentiality
- Listen to pupils' views and involve them in drawing up anti-bullying policies.

CHIPS

ChildLine is at the forefront of the fight against bullying. Through its helpline and ChildLine In Partnership with Schools (CHIPS) programme, the charity has built up extensive experience of helping schools and children to deal with bullying. CHIPS was launched in 1998 and has proved extremely successful in bringing young people together to challenge problems like bullying in school.

ChildLine also publishes practical leaflets (for both children and parents) about how to tackle bullying, produces research reports and works with policy-makers on how schools can minimise bullying.

WHAT PUPILS CAN DO AT SCHOOL

Children and young people at school can take an active part in helping to tackle the problem of bullying. This includes:

- becoming a mediator
- becoming a buddy
- getting involved in mentoring projects – ChildLine's CHIPS programme trains children and young adults to become peer mentors
- using a bully box – where written reports of bullying are posted for mediators and/or staff to read
- taking part in circle times – discuss issues within class
- getting involved in Bully Courts – a council of pupils who have responsibility for creating and policing a school's anti-bullying policy
- addressing anger management – counselling and/or therapy
- keeping records in an incident book – for bullies, bystanders and victims to use
- conducting termly anonymous surveys – to assess bullying within the school.

Look at the Anti-Bullying Network website (the section on Young People) to find ways of tackling bullying and for information on peer support and buddy schemes. Some secondary schools have peer counselling/listening schemes, where young people are trained by adults to support other young people who are having problems. If your teacher needs some advice about initiating a peer support scheme at your school, ask them to visit the ChildLine website or the section on School Staff on the Anti-Bullying Network website.

SMILE

Dunoon Grammar School in Scotland runs a peer support group called SMILE, which stands for Sixth Year Make Issues Less Extreme. Volunteers for the group are trained in June ready to start in August. SMILE members:

- wear yellow smiley badges and are to be found in busy/problem areas (or hotspots) at break times
- act as shepherds for new S1 (first-year) pupils during their first week at secondary school. This includes escorting them to and collecting them from classes. SMILE members can spot problems quickly and deal with them or pass them on to staff
- visit, where possible, Personal and Social Education and the ten-minute morning Form period (administration and registration)
- run a lunchtime games/chat club
- service an internal mail system, which helps contact from pupils with bullying issues, etc.
- raise funds for ChildLine
- run a buddy service for vulnerable pupils
- organise a poster competition during the S1 Playfair Day (an event for all first-year pupils to explore tolerance, prejudice, bullying, working together, etc.)
- help organise discos and other functions
- encourage and help pupils affected by bullying, etc. to join clubs and friendship groups.

Having a peer support group such as this in every school would be a huge asset and would really help children and young people to feel confident at school. You could show this information to your teacher or other member of staff who may be interested in starting a similar group in your school.

'MAKE THE DIFFERENCE'

The year 2004 marked the beginning of a new initiative by the DfES (Department for Education and Skills): they are holding a series of anti-bullying conferences called Make the Difference around the country, which are attended by pupils, parents and teachers. The aim of these conferences is to highlight the fact that schools will no longer tolerate bullying and will be taking practical steps to deal with it. You can look at the DfES website for more information.

WHAT IF BULLYING HAPPENS OUTSIDE SCHOOL?

It is not the legal responsibility of the school to deal with bullying that occurs outside school, even if the people concerned are wearing school uniform. Most school principals will want to know if children from their school are causing distress on their way to and from school, but don't automatically assume that they should have to resolve the problem. In this case it may be necessary to get the community police involved. This doesn't mean there has to be any legal action taken, so don't be intimidated by approaching the police if you feel desperate. You could even ask the school to get the community police to come in and give a talk in assembly about offensive behaviour and its consequences.

If legal action is considered, take account of the time and cost this entails. Legal action is time-consuming, expensive and difficult. The Anti-Bullying Network has an information sheet, also available on their website, which discusses the pros and cons of involving a solicitor.

If bullying is taking place on the bus to and from school it may be possible for you – or someone else on your behalf – to discuss the possibility of a bus monitor system with the school. The local bus service may even want to get involved. Bus monitors can help to reduce bullying and vandalism on buses.

If you are being bullied by someone from your school on the way home, then another strategy the school could adopt is to keep the perpetrators at school for a set amount of time after school has finished. This would then give you enough time to get home safely. Alternatively, arrange to have someone go with you to and from school, such as a parent, relative or group of friends. There is always a greater feeling of safety in numbers.

WHAT IF YOU HAVE A FRIEND WHO IS BEING BULLIED?

Sometimes you may find yourself in a situation where a friend, or even someone you don't really know, is being bullied and it makes you feel really uncomfortable. What should you do? First of all, refuse to participate in the bullying. If you don't join in it shows the bully that you don't agree with what s/he's doing; it shows the other group members that it is possible to stand up to the ringleader; and it gives the sufferer a ray of hope.

'A few of my friends were being bullied at school by this group of girls from the same year as us. They came to me and asked me for help. I don't know why they asked me, I'd never been a bully or threatened people, but I was tall and quite punky – maybe they thought that would intimidate them a bit. Anyway, together, with me at the front, we went and confronted these girls. I felt really nervous, but determined to put a stop to the bullying. I told them to leave my friends alone, not in an attacking way, but quite assertively, and amazingly they did.'

Emma, 21

IS THERE SUCH A THING AS AN INNOCENT BYSTANDER?

Never ignore someone being bullied. If you do you'll only feel worried or guilty. It is often very useful if bystanders come forward, because they can tell someone or verify what has happened.

Allowing a case of bullying to occur without trying to do something constructive about it is like giving the bully permission to continue. You can assess the situation and decide whether just making the bully aware of the fact that he or she is doing something wrong will end the problem, but never rush over and challenge the bully – it might make things worse and the bully might turn on you as well. The best thing you can do is to inform a teacher or another adult immediately. You can do it discreetly and ask the teacher not to mention your name if you're worried about reprisals.

If you are aware of a case of bullying, but you feel worried about telling someone, perhaps you could write an anonymous letter to the teacher. Do you have a bully box at school where you could post your letter? If you are still worried, perhaps you could ask another friend or adult to do it for you.

Ways of helping

You could try and make friends with the person who is being bullied. Often people who are bullied have very low self-esteem and knowing that you want to be a friend will mean a lot. This doesn't mean you have to spend all your time together, it could just mean a friendly chat when you see each other and making sure they know you will support them if any trouble arises.

The bully may also have few real friends – he or she may also have personal problems. Being a friend to the bully may provide an opportunity for them to talk about their problems. You may feel that it's impossible for you to offer friendship to the bully. This is completely understandable if you have been bullied by this person, but just responding kindly to them may be enough to encourage them to stop bullying.

'It wasn't until I found out how Joe felt that I realised what effect I was having on him. I guess I just enjoyed all the other kids laughing at what I was saying. I didn't stop to think how Joe might be feeling. I don't think I really cared at the time.'

Luke, 12

HOW DO YOU STOP BEING A BULLY?

Children who get away with aggressive or criminal behaviour often go on to be criminals as adults. If you have been bullying it's very important that you find ways to stop, not just for the people you bully, but for yourself as well.

Bullying can lead to exclusion from school, and missing out on your education could affect you later when you're looking for a job.

Think about your reasons for bullying (look at the list in Chapter 2 (page 13)). Were you bullied by an older brother or sister? Did this feel humiliating? Are you angry with him/her for making you feel like this? Does it make you feel small? Do you bully other people so that other people can feel as bad or worse than you do? Are you trying to pass on your anger?

Do you call other kids hurtful names because it gets you lots of attention? Do you force others to become 'friends' with you because they'd be too scared not to? Do you go round with a gang that bullies people because you want to fit in and not be picked on yourself?

If you want to stop bullying, you can:
- apologise – either orally or in writing
- talk to someone you trust
- get counselling – the best way to do this may be family counselling, especially if you feel that you are being bullied at home
- learn how to control your anger
- take up a sport such as judo or karate
- get involved in an activity that really interests you
- set goals, e.g. stay out of the way of people you've bullied, walk away if you feel angry and don't allow anyone else to encourage you to bully.

The first step is to acknowledge that you have a problem with bullying and need to get some help. Speak to someone you trust, such as a parent, teacher, relation, friend of the family or even one of the people you've been bullying. Explain what drives you to bully and how it makes you feel and that you want to stop. Ask the person you have bullied how it made them feel and apologise for causing them distress. Don't expect them to forgive you, but apologising will help them to realise that it wasn't their fault and that the bullying will now stop. They might even decide to help you find ways to stop being a bully.

You could contact an organisation such as ChildLine and Kidscape. They are there to help people who want to stop bullying as well as those who are being bullied. They can offer you useful advice and may be able to help you with any problems that have led you to start bullying.

It is really helpful to find something that you are really good at or really enjoy. This will help you to feel good about yourself and help you stop feeling the need to put others down.

Remember: treat others the way you would like to be treated yourself.

Other useful information on how to overcome bullying, such as ways of coping with your anger, can be found in Chapter 6.

---

1 *Your friend Dylan is being bullied by another boy in his class, who uses physical threats to get Dylan to hand over his pocket money. You're at Dylan's house when his mum asks Dylan for the £10 he owes her for the CD she got him. Dylan says he's lost his money. What do you do?*

a Tell his mum the truth.

b Say nothing – you don't want the bully picking on you as well.

c Talk to Dylan alone and tell him he has to tell his mum the truth – it's not fair that he should get into trouble, and if it's not sorted out now, then the bully will only do it again.

The best thing you can do is to persuade Dylan to speak to his mum. He might feel scared to speak to her, but if he warns his mum that he is telling her in strictest confidence then hopefully the problem will be sorted out.

2 *You are running across the playground and someone who's not looking bumps into you and knocks you over. Do you:*

a Get up, call him stupid and punch him hard, then kick him to the ground?

b Burst into tears and bury your face?

c Look at the person who knocked you over and wait for an apology. If they don't apologise, ask them to.

Everyone has accidents, but it's reasonable to expect an apology. If the person doesn't apologise, you could ask them to do so. There is no point being abusive and aggressive – it was only an accident and they didn't mean to hurt you.

CHAPTER FIVE:

THE EFFECTS OF BULLYING
What the results can be

ChildLine estimates that 16 children a year commit suicide because they have been bullied.

Source: ChildLine

HOW DO YOU FEEL WHEN YOU'RE BULLIED?

Being bullied can make you feel scared and hurt. It can also make you feel that there is something wrong with you and that it is your fault. Remember: IT IS NOT YOUR FAULT.

The reason people bully is to make someone feel scared, upset, angry, anxious and helpless. If the person being bullied does not feel or show any of these feelings, then the bully has not achieved the result s/he wanted. Eventually they will have to give up.

LINDA'S STORY

'I was bullied at school by the person who was supposed to be my best friend. It was very subtle and started by Sophie spreading

rumours about me and getting our mutual "friends" to run away from me. This was when I was about 11 or 12. The worst bit was that she was so clever and devious that I didn't know it was her that was doing it. I can remember one day telling some friends how excited I was that my mum was pregnant again. Suddenly they all said, "BABIES!" and ran away from me laughing. This was of course at Sophie's instruction. Apparently she'd told them I was dull and boring and it was all I talked to her about. Around this time people also started calling me "sheep" which was because she'd said my hair was so dry it was like straw.

'I can remember pretending to be ill so I didn't have to go to school, but I never managed to get away with it.

'My up-and-down relationship with Sophie got worse as we got older. When we became interested in boys she would tell them personal stuff about me. I was wise to her now, but I didn't stand up for myself – I just reacted to whatever her mood was. She had an incredibly sharp tongue, was very popular, was allowed to have little parties every weekend, and had very liberal parents.

'I remember thinking that there was something truly wrong with me and spent hours trying to work out what it was. I went on numerous diets, frequently wrestled with my appearance, blamed my parents for not being like hers. Around this time I became fed up with my life and started drinking and smoking puff. Looking back I think it was reacting to the feelings of self-loathing that Sophie instilled in me. I didn't know what she felt about me or why she did these things to me, so I thought the problem was in me rather than with her.

'I stopped seeing her when we went our separate ways after secondary school. She has appeared in my dreams ever since then.

When I'm unsure of someone, don't trust them or if I'm feeling persecuted, Sophie will always pop up. She doesn't, however, affect my conscious life any more, my self-esteem grew the moment she wasn't in my life.'   **Linda, 27**

Being bullied can make you feel:
- lonely and isolated
- over-conscious of something you are being bullied about (e.g. weight, height, freckles, stammer, etc.)
- unable to socialise and make friends
- that people won't like you or that they will bully you too.

Symptoms of bullying
These stories were provided by ChildLine.

Jackie, 14, was desperately upset when she called ChildLine. A girl who used to be her best friend had turned against her and was now calling her names and making her life 'hell'. Jackie said: 'I took an overdose a couple of months ago. I just wanted someone to notice me – to notice the bullying.'

Robert, 11, rang from a phone box saying that he was being bullied by a group of boys at his school. 'It's been going on for three years now. None of my teachers will do anything to stop it – when they do tell the boys off, the bullies are even worse than before.' Robert said that recently he had pretended to be ill so that he could be sent home from school. He was now beginning to worry that he would fall behind with his schoolwork. 'I just want it to stop,' he said.

Bullying can lead to:
- withdrawal

- school phobia
- stress-induced physical symptoms such as headaches and stomach aches
- falling behind at school – academic standards dropping
- unhappiness
- anxiety
- feelings of isolation
- difficulty sleeping
- bullying somebody else
- depression
- agoraphobia
- eating disorders
- using alcohol and/or drugs
- self-harm
- feeling suicidal.

> **For a closer look at some of the issues listed above, see these other titles in the *Real Life Issues* series: *Eating Disorders, Addictions* and *Coping with Life*.**

Staying away from school

When you are facing a difficult time at school, it can be a terrifying place to have to go to and you may find all sorts of reasons not to go. You may even want to play truant. The problem with taking time off school is that it can then be even harder to go back, and you can also fall behind with your work, which will lead to further stress.

TIM'S STORY

'I was being bullied at secondary school. I was in fear of travelling to and from school because this boy would try and humiliate me, calling me names, punching the top of my arm, and he jumped on top of

me one time with some of his mates on the playing fields and gave me a black eye. I had to tell my mum and dad that a cricket ball had hit me, because my dad had a tendency to flare up and he would have gone ballistic. He was in the year below me, but he had these two really hard brothers who were also known for being bullies – in fact the whole family were notorious bullies on the estate where I lived. So I started bunking off school because of the fear of his two older brothers. The boy who was bullying me was using his notoriety to bully me and others as well. I feel that it really put me off school and I ended being off a lot just prior to my exams when we were supposed to be revising our work. In the end I only turned up for some of my exams and I put no real effort into it, because I'd lost all impetus in my school work.'
Tim, 25

Moods

Depression can describe a variety of moods, from occasionally feeling low-spirited to intense feelings of worthlessness and guilt and feeling that life is not worth living. Symptoms include sleeping a lot, or not being able to get to sleep, eating a lot, or hardly wanting to eat, a loss of interest in things in general and finding it hard to do things.

Alcohol/drug dependency

If you are using drink and/or drugs to help you cope and to escape reality then you really have reached crisis point and you need help. Alcohol or drugs may seem like a way of blocking out the grim realities, but they will only make your problems worse, by making you feel depressed, insecure or paranoid.

'I used to wake up in the morning and get the bottle of vodka from underneath my bed and have a drink before I went to school. I wanted to block out my fear.'
Linda, 27

Psychological injury

Sometimes the effects of bullying can lead to post-traumatic stress disorder, which can make you unable to articulate what has gone on. Don't give up: seek help and after a time you will be able to work on resolving your problems.

Eating disorders

If you have an eating disorder, it's really important to speak to someone before you end up becoming really ill. Most young people with eating disorders first confide in a close friend. If you tell someone your problems, they can help you get advice, e.g. from ChildLine, or talk to your parents or caregiver for you. Eating disorders are not confined to girls: boys shouldn't feel ashamed to talk about their problems. Boys often prefer to talk to their parents, caregiver or doctor first.

'At school I was always teased by other girls in the class for being fat. I started to go and throw up in the toilet after I ate, and then I tried avoiding eating altogether. I ended up in hospital.'

Francesca, 14

Destructive thoughts

Suicidal feelings as a result of bullying are not uncommon. If you are having suicidal thoughts or wanting to self-harm then this is very serious indeed and you MUST get help immediately. If you can't talk to your parents, talk to a friend, talk to your doctor, talk to ChildLine. No one should have to go through what you're feeling on their own. It is essential that you tell your family and friends what is going on. There are plenty of people who have felt the same as you do right now, who have come out the other side and who have gone on to live fulfilling and happy lives. PLEASE ask for help.

Bullying can be responsible for serious psychological injuries that can continue into adult life if not dealt with.

WHAT ABOUT THE LONG TERM?

The long-term effects on children and young people who have been bullied vary a great deal. With the support of friends and trusted adults, most will come through their experiences with no lasting effects.

The outlook for the bully is not good. If the problem is not diagnosed and dealt with, criminality and delinquency are more likely to occur and relationships with both friends and partners will be harder to maintain. You can choose to take action now! (See Chapter 4 for advice on ways to stop bullying.)

---

1 *These kids at school keep saying you're fat and it's really upsetting you. Do you:*

a Start dieting like crazy to lose weight and sometimes starve yourself or make yourself sick?

b Talk to your parents and/or doctor to discuss positive ways of building up your confidence?

c Ignore these people. They are stupid and rude.

d Say to the bullies: 'I'm not the slightest bit concerned about what you think of my weight. I only want to be friends with people who are mature, not childish, superficial and ignorant.'

People who call you rude names are just not worth knowing. It might be that they don't really realise how upset you are by what they say, so you could try telling them how you feel. The best thing to do is (b), (c) or (d). Don't ever consider dieting unless you've discussed it with your

---

parents first, and never starve yourself or make yourself sick. If you have started to do this, seek help straightaway – starving or vomiting is a serious risk to your health.

2 *You feel really depressed. You have been emotionally and physically bullied for years and you see no way out. Your mother is really worried about you and wants to help. Do you:*

a Stay locked in your bedroom – you don't want to see anyone right now?

b Carry on as normal, but focus on the day when you can leave school?

c Accept your mother's offer of help and speak to someone at ChildLine?

Depression is really hard to deal with because it makes everything seem so difficult – we just feel like crawling into a hole and staying there. Giving yourself a focus can help, e.g. only three months left before you leave school, so every day you're getting nearer; work hard for your exams because you want to go to university and study law; you are going to become a famous artist and show them all. If anyone offers you help, take it, even if you don't think you can face it. You are depressed because of external circumstances (the bullying) and you can be helped.

CHAPTER SIX:

OVERCOMING BULLYING
You can get through it

EMOTIONS

The emotional scars that result from bullying are far worse than the physical scars and they can have serious long-term effects on your life. How often have you heard the advice, walk tall, act confident and pretend that you're not bothered about the name-calling? Well, this is all good advice, but wouldn't it be great if you actually *did* feel confident in yourself?

Bullying attacks your confidence and your self-esteem, leaving you less able to defend yourself both emotionally and physically, and causing you to become even more vulnerable. So how do we stop this happening? It's all about changing the way you view a situation and your responses to it.

ANGER

Dealing with anger constructively

If you are bullied you will feel angry, but if you react angrily at the time the whole situation can get out of control: the bully may become

TIP BOX

FAMOUS PEOPLE WHO HAVE BEEN BULLIED

Phill Jupitus (comedian and DJ), Ozzy Osbourne (rock musician), Kate Winslet (actress), Tom Cruise (actor), Julian Clary (comedian and TV presenter), Michelle Williams (Destiny's Child), Jacobi Shaddix (Papa Roach), Billy Connolly (comedian), Daryl Hannah (actress), Neil Kinnock (politician), Frank Bruno (boxer), Dudley Moore (actor), Jo O'Meara and Bradley (S Club), Sir Ranulph Fiennes (polar explorer), Jo Brand (comedian), Michelle Pfeiffer (actress), Alan Davies (comedian), Patsy Palmer (actress), Stevie Wonder (musician), Harrison Ford (actor), Duncan Goodhew (Olympic Gold Medal swimmer), Whoopi Goldberg (actress), Will Smith (R 'n' B artist and actor), the Prince of Wales (you know who he is, don't you!) and so on and so on ...

As you can see, there is life after bullying. All these celebrities have endured painful experiences and come through the other side to live successful lives. You can too.

more aggressive; or you might end up being labelled the bully. What usually happens is that your anger is bottled up and suppressed, you become depressed and anxious and your self-esteem suffers. People who are bullied often have angry outbursts, which end up getting them into trouble and their self-esteem suffers even more as a result. It's a downward spiral.

You can't pretend that you don't feel angry when you do, but you need to find a way of unleashing the power of anger in a constructive way. When you experience feelings of anger, recognise these feelings. Try to give yourself some space so that you can think about your reaction and the possible consequences of your actions. Use your anger in a positive way rather than being aggressive or bottling it up. It may be that you will just express your feelings either aloud or to yourself.

The same applies to people who bully. Controlling your anger so that you don't end up hurting or upsetting another person is all about having the ability to admit your feelings of anger and understand why you are feeling that way (e.g. 'I'm angry because my father drinks too much and then comes home and shouts and swears at me. He threatens me and hits me and makes me feel unloved'). If you can understand what it is that makes you feel angry, you can begin to understand why you bully. If you can understand what motivates you to bully, then you can understand why you should stop what you're doing. You're shouting and swearing and threatening a kid in class, because that's what your father does to you – you're trying to transfer your anger to someone else.

These are some negative ways of expressing your anger:
- swearing

- shouting
- losing your temper
- threatening
- violence
- being over-critical
- shaming
- coldness
- rejection.

Give yourself space to work out how best to respond to your feelings of anger in a constructive way by:
- taking five deep breaths
- counting to ten in whatever language you choose
- thinking of ten things, e.g. girls' names, flowers, footballers
- walking away from the situation or person who is making you feel angry.

Releasing anger

If you are angry this is the way you feel and you don't need to justify why you feel angry. Your feelings are your own. Anger is an important and powerful emotion.

Anger is often linked to the way someone else has behaved or treated you, which means that you have someone to blame. But once you start blaming someone else for your feelings of anger you are allowing them to gain control over your feelings. This is a handing over of power. This means you are not in control. Take back that power. Convert your natural feelings of anger into positive action.

We all need to let off steam now and again, and when we're angry we feel a huge amount of energy, which needs to be released. A friend of mine finds that picking up his guitar and pumping out some songs is pure therapy. You could play your favourite music really loud and jump around to it, play a game of football or tennis, go for a run, write an angry letter or use a simple relaxation technique such as tensing and relaxing every muscle in your body.

When you've cooled down, think about what has made you so cross. Think about who you are actually cross with. What happens with anger is that we tend to want to pass it on. If you've been bullied by your big brother at home, you might try to pass your anger on by bullying someone at school. If you've been bullied at school you may go home and shout at your little sister or give your mum a hard time. You'll hear many parents say, 'I was really cross with my husband/wife, but s/he wasn't there, so I spent all evening snapping at the children'. We often pass our anger on to people who haven't even done anything wrong.

We also use anger to cover up other emotions. If something goes wrong for us, we try to find something or someone to blame. It's just so easy – it's not our fault – something or someone else is to blame – we are powerless. But that's the problem: if we're powerless we don't have control; if we don't have control we can't sort out the problem for ourselves. We cannot be proactive while we blame others.

'I felt angry because when I started this new school this girl called Shannon kept putting me down. She kept criticising the way I dressed, the way my hair was not cool, the way I always answered questions in class, the way I didn't answer questions in class.'

Max, 14

'I used to be best friends with this girl called Lucy, but she went away for three weeks to Trinidad. While she was away, I made friends with

*another girl in our class called Yas, as she didn't have anyone to play
with. When Lucy came back my mum told me to make sure Lucy
didn't feel left out. Actually, what happened was that Lucy and Yas
became best friends and I was either ignored, spoken really grumpily
to, whispered about or bossed around. It made me feel really upset
and at home I kept having these really angry outbursts and no one
understood what was going on.'*

Sophie, 13

Understanding why you feel angry can help you discover what would
make you feel better and what you need to do to sort out the
situation. For example, 'I'm angry with my boyfriend because he was
supposed to call me last night to arrange a trip to the cinema, but by
the time he called the film had already started.' How would you
respond? Passively, aggressively or assertively? (See Chapter 3.)

The way we deal with our anger is generally part of our conditioning. If
your parents or caregiver shout, swear and slam doors when they are
angry, it's likely that you will too. If they take a deep breath and then
try to work out how to deal with the problem, you probably will too.
We tend to follow the example set by our caregivers, because these
are the people from whom we learn how to deal with our emotions.

Of course, if we are scared of our parents' anger, we may be too
frightened to show ours – and this has a negative impact too.
Remember that your parents learnt their emotional responses from the
examples set by their parents. Dealing with emotion may be
particularly hard for parents who didn't have a parent to learn from.

It's also important to understand that anger is not just a negative thing.
Anger is a very powerful emotion and produces a huge amount of

energy. Sometimes anger drives us to achieve and become successful:

■ anger is power
■ anger can help you reach further and achieve goals
■ anger can help you overcome your fears.

'All through my childhood, I never once remember my parents praising me. All they ever did was be sarcastic to me, put me down and criticise me all the time. It wasn't just to me, they did it to my brothers and sisters too. It was just the way they were, but it made me feel they didn't respect me, they weren't proud of me and I felt unappreciated. It was really this that drove me to become really good at what I did, writing music, because I wanted to prove them wrong and for them to see I had worth.'

Tim, 21

'My teacher was always dissing me and trying to humiliate me in front of the class. She also said I would never pass my exams. It made me so angry that I studied really hard and ended up getting really good grades.'

Sally, 16

'We played football at the weekend and one of the players from the other team fouled one of my team-mates just as he was about to score a goal. He had blood coming out of his leg and everything. It made me so angry but also determined to win. You should have seen me after that. My dad said he'd never seen me play so well.'

Robert, 14

If you feel angry, remember that anger can be a hugely powerful and important emotion, and anger can help you overcome your fear.

Hot potatoes

When a bully is verbally abusing you, try to think, 'He (or she) is angry (for whatever reason) and he's trying to pass his anger on to me. The anger is his feeling, not mine, and I won't let him pass it on to me.' Imagine that his anger is a hot potato and in your mind pass it back to him.

When the other members of the gang torment you, try to think, 'These bullies are trying to frighten me because they are frightened of the ringleader. They are frightened that if they don't stick with the crowd they'll be picked on. I won't let their feelings of fear be passed on to me.' Visualise their feelings of fear as a hot potato and throw it back to them.

FACING FEAR

There are two different ways to view fear:
- fear is like a wall or blockade, preventing you from moving forward
- fear is a challenge.

If you are being bullied you will no doubt be feeling very frightened. Don't try and push this emotion away or pretend that it doesn't exist. Allow yourself to feel the fear, but also try to understand it. Fear can hold us back in many ways. It can prevent us from talking to someone we are in awe of, taking up a challenge or accepting a fantastic opportunity. Fear can stop us becoming truly fulfilled. Facing up to fear can help us feel the power of courage, which can make us feel good about ourselves

How to cope with fear

Here are a few tips.
- Try focusing on your breathing, so that each breath is slow, deep and controlled. This will have a calming effect.

■ Try transferring your fear by writing down what it is you are frightened about or use something that can hold your fears for you, such as a worry doll. A worry doll is particularly useful at night: you can tell it your fears and then put it under your pillow so that the doll can look after them while you sleep.

■ Try alternative remedies. Homeopathy or flower remedies can help alleviate the problems associated with fear. You can get information on alternative remedies at the library, but you must discuss this first with your parent or caregiver. The best course of action would be to visit a practitioner. This does cost money, but it might be worth it.

■ Try visualisation. You could visualise a protective light around yourself or a guardian angel looking down on you. You could even visualise your bully as someone who is really very vulnerable (especially if you suspect they are also being bullied). Whatever works for you.

If you can understand the reasons why someone is bullying you, and the kind of responses they want, you can also try and find ways to resolve the problem so that the bullying doesn't work. This gives *you* power over the situation, not the bully.

'They were always saying mean things to me about my hair. At first I wanted to get my hair cut, but then I realised that if it wasn't my hair it would be about something else. I realised they just wanted to pick on someone and I just happened to be there. I'm a sensitive person, but I decided not to take what they had to say personally and then it couldn't affect me.'

Simon, 11

Simon realised that the bullies were able to get at him because they knew he was sensitive. He realised that the real issue wasn't his hair –

they were just trying to find something to pick on because they wanted to upset him. As soon as he understood that, he knew how to respond differently to their jibes in a way that made their verbal abuse ineffective. Although we can't control the way other people behave around us, we can control how we respond, and with bullying, this is often the most fundamental thing to address.

A POSITIVE ATTITUDE

Being positive is all to do with how you interpret what happens to you. Life is what you make it, not something you have to endure. It is very easy for us to lose a sense of proportion and make molehills into mountains. Instead of getting upset or depressed by an argument with a friend or not winning at football, work out ways of reuniting your friendship and be determined to train even harder for the next match.

If we become too bogged down with what's not going right in our lives, we end up being unable to see all the good things that are happening.

This is all very easy to say, of course, and it might be very hard to see the good in your life when bullying feels like it's taking over. Trying to think about what you can learn from your experiences to get through and deal with the problem is a positive step.

Think about the things in your life that you like and can feel good about, for example people or pets you love, hobbies you enjoy. Think about what you have that's good in your life and feel love and appreciation, rather than feeling negative about what you don't have.

Take up some form of exercise. Whether it's martial arts or brisk walking, make sure it's something you enjoy. Choose a form of exercise that doesn't involve having to achieve certain goals, like losing a pound a week or doing 30 lengths every time you go swimming. Do the exercise purely for enjoyment – it will help you feel good about yourself.

Another great way of relieving negative feelings is to enjoy a comedy programme. Find something funny to watch or listen to as regularly as you can. Laughing is therapeutic and will help you relax. Even better if you can watch the programme with your family – it's great to enjoy a laugh together. By the same token, avoid watching things that make you feel unhappy or depressed, such as certain documentary subjects or the news, at least until you feel more able to deal with it.

Just trying to maintain a positive attitude will have an effect on your body language. You will have decided to take steps to overcome the bullying and you will look and feel more confident and assertive.

Nobody's perfect

It's true – no one is perfect. We are all different – and the best way to feel good about ourselves is to accept the way we are made and make the best out of it. Look at yourself in the mirror and look at yourself as you are, not in comparison to someone you would rather look like. Look at what it is that's great about you, and learn to love yourself, warts and all. So what if you think your bottom is too big, if you love yourself unconditionally, you will nurture your self-esteem and will enable yourself to reach your potential.

Don't put yourself down

Even if you've been put down for years by people at school, friends or relations, never put yourself down. Don't criticise yourself or make jokes at your own expense. This will not only affect your perception of yourself and lower your self-esteem and confidence, it will also affect the way other people see you. A friend of mine went out with a man who she thought was the bee's knees, but he was always putting himself down. Eventually this girl's perception of him changed and she no longer found him attractive. So don't say, 'I can never get things right', 'I'm no good at that', or, 'I'm so stupid' – even if you may be thinking it – because it will affect the way others view you.

I'm great

Write a list of all the things about yourself that you like:

- I am good at ... e.g. cooking, writing stories, making people laugh, remembering things ...
- I am kind, honest, caring, nurturing, empathetic, supportive ...
- I have lovely eyes, gorgeous freckles, a happy smile, beautiful skin ...

Then write down a list of things that you like about your life. For example, I have:

- a great mum/dad
- a brilliant friend
- a lovely bedroom
- a super camera
- a fantastic comedy film to watch ...

If you can, get your family and/or a friend to write down a list of what they like about you, and what they think is great about your life. They might draw attention to something about you or your life that you hadn't even considered. Look at this list if you're ever feeling down about yourself or your life. It will be a great way to remind yourself how fabulous you really are.

Express yourself

You can use your experiences of bullying in a creative way. This will actively help you deal with the trauma and upset of bullying. You can do this through artwork – drawing, painting or sculpture – or writing.

You could draw a picture of yourself, expressing the way you are feeling by the colours you use, the clothes you are wearing, the environment you are in, or other people, animals or pets that you include in the picture. You will actually be able to see how you feel when you look at the picture.

You can use a diary or notebook to write down what has happened to you – what they did, when they did it, who was involved and who witnessed what was going on. Remember to date the bullying in case you ever need to refer back to it. Write down how you felt when it was going on, afterwards and how you feel when you are writing it. If you have spoken to anyone about the incident, include that in your writing too: how did they respond? What did they do? Were you happy about it?

Another good way of expressing yourself is by writing a story or poem based on your own experiences of being bullied. Story writing will help to release your unconscious mind and help you to work out your problems. Who knows, you might even get it published one day!

You could even write a letter to the perpetrator. This gives you a chance to say what you want. You don't need to post the letter, just get your feelings out on that piece of paper. It is amazingly therapeutic.

Seeing or reading how you feel is a positive step because it means you are taking an active part in dealing with your situation by expressing yourself – releasing your feelings rather than bottling them up. It also means you can look at your feelings objectively. Expressing your feelings is hugely important, because even if you tell someone about your experiences of bullying, you might not always tell them how it made you feel.

WHAT HAPPENS WHEN THE BULLYING HAS STOPPED?

Even when the bullying stops you may still feel anger or hatred for the bully and what he/she has done to you. This is completely natural, but it does mean that your life is continuing to be affected by someone who has bullied you in the past. Don't allow them to have this control over your life. Hatred prevents you getting free from the pain of what has happened to you in the past and it can affect your pleasure in life. You need to rid yourself of this hatred so that you can take full pleasure in the here and now and move on with your life. In order for you to do this you will need to be able to forgive the perpetrator/s. This might seem like an impossible task, but it's worth a try for your own happiness.

Ridding hatred from your life

Write down all the things the bully did to you on a piece of paper. Read it back to yourself and allow yourself to feel the emotions that rise to the surface when you do. Don't force them down or stop yourself crying. When you feel ready, tell yourself that these experiences are in the past, where they belong, and that you forgive the person who did them. Then destroy the piece of paper. Burn the paper and imagine that your feelings of hatred are being burnt, too.

It may also be very helpful to get some form of counselling.

MAKING FRIENDS

Being bullied affects your confidence and self-esteem, and this can have a knock-on effect when you are trying to make friends. Kidscape asked a group of 13-year-olds to come up with a list of what they liked about their friends. Their responses are listed below:

Good friends:
- show an interest in what people do
- are good at giving compliments without going overboard
- go around with a pleasant expression on their face
- laugh at people's jokes
- are kind
- ask, not demand, to join in
- offer to help others with work or to carry things
- invite people to do something
- hang around places where other students are
- are welcoming to new students
- are good at thinking of something interesting to do
- are willing to share
- are humorous and tell jokes
- are fair
- are good at organising games or activities.

The group was then asked to think about characteristics that would not make a good friend. They came up with these:
- being bossy
- telling others how to behave
- telling others they are doing things wrong
- talking about yourself all the time
- being mean

- talking about other people behind their back
- being negative and sarcastic
- being too intense or serious all the time
- bragging
- moaning all the time
- being a bully
- claiming credit for something you didn't do
- lying or cheating.

Think about the qualities that make a good friend and try to work on them. You are probably most of these already, but bullying may have made you doubt yourself. Don't worry, you're bound to feel a little nervous or shy. Remember, everyone is unique and everyone is special, so put on a happy face and take the plunge. Go up to someone you'd like to be friends with at school (they don't have to be in the same year) and start off a conversation – did you see that programme on TV last night? Have you heard so-and-so's new single? What do you think of it? What sort of music do you like? Have you done your homework? Did you find that bit about the green onions difficult? I think I know your sister. I like your hairstyle/bag/shoes. What book are you reading? Do you live in such and such a street? You get my bus, don't you? Or just simply, How are you? People love to talk about themselves. Not everyone will be pleasant back, but you won't know unless you try, and there are lots of really lovely people out there.

If you know someone else in your school who has been having a hard time with bullying, they would probably really appreciate your friendship. Their experiences of bullying may make them a little distrustful of you, but persevere and they'll soon realise you are genuine.

'If anyone who is reading this now is being bullied, remember this, things do get better. You won't be bullied for the rest of your life. You can come out the other side. If I did it, so can you.'

Ashley, 19

FINAL WORD

'My advice would be to make good friends who will respect you, follow your dreams – help other people who are being bullied and remember it's not forever.'

Tim, 21

DIRECTORY

HELPLINES AND CHATLINES

ANTI BULLYING CAMPAIGN HELPLINE
Tel: 020 7378 1446
Open Monday to Friday 9.30am to 5.30pm.

BULLYING ONLINE
Email: help@bullying.co.uk
You can email 24 hours a day, 365 days a year. If you don't have access to a computer at home, you can email from school with your home postal address for a written response.

CHILDLINE
Tel: 0800 1111
Website: www.childline.org.uk
Completely free and confidential. Call any time of the day or night, any day of the year. Trained volunteer counsellors comfort, advise

and protect children and young people. Lines can be busy – but KEEP TRYING.

CHILDLINE SCOTLAND – BULLYING HELPLINE
Tel: 0800 441111
Open to children and young people calling from anywhere in Scotland between 3.30pm and 9.30pm.

KIDSCAPE HELPLINE
Tel: 020 7730 3300
Open Monday to Wednesday, 9.30am to 5.30pm.

SAMARITANS
Tel: 08457 909090 (UK); 1850 60 90 90 (Republic of Ireland)
Email: jo@samaritans.org

STANDING TALL
Email: dafydd@standingtall.org.uk
Website: www.standingtall.org.uk
Internet chatline.

USEFUL ORGANISATIONS

BULLYING ONLINE
Website: www.bullying.co.uk
Advice for pupils, school projects and parents; legal advice.

CHILDLINE IN PARTNERSHIP WITH SCHOOLS (CHIPS)
Tel: 020 7650 3200

EDUCATION OTHERWISE
PO Box 7420
London N9 9SG
Website: www.education-otherwise.org
Information on home education.

KIDSCAPE
2 Grosvenor Gardens
London SW1 0DH
Website: www.kidscape.org.uk

LEICESTER LESBIAN GAY AND BISEXUAL CENTRE
15 Wellington Street
Leicester LE1 6HH
Tel: 0116 254 7412 helpline: 0116 255 0667
Provides training, advice, support and counselling for young people.
Runs First Out, a lesbian, gay and bisexual youth group.

SCOTTISH CHILD LAW CENTRE
Tel: 0900 328 8970
Freephone advice service for under-18s. Open 9.30am to 4pm,
except Thursdays when it is open from 6pm to 7.30pm.

SCHOOLHOUSE HOME EDUCATION ASSOCIATION
311 Perth Road
Dundee DD2 1LG 01382 646964
Website: www.home-education.org.uk

TOWER HAMLETS COLLEGE
Learning Centre
Poplar High Street
LONDON
E14 0AF

For parents

Children's Legal Centre (England)
Tel: 01206 873820
Open Monday to Friday, 2pm–5pm.

KIDSCAPE
Helpline for parents of children who are being bullied. Open Monday to Friday, 10am–4pm.
Tel: 08451 205 204

MOSAC (MOTHERS OF SEXUALLY ABUSED CHILDREN)
Tel: 0800 980 1958

PARENTLINE PLUS
Tel: 0808 800 2222

Websites

www.dfes.gov.uk/bullying
Make the Difference conference details.

PUBLICATIONS

Courage to Care: Submission on homophobic bullying, Leicester Lesbian and Gay Action
Website: http://freespace.virgin.net/lesgay.action/courage.html

Trotman's Real Life Issues series. Self-help books offering information and advice on a range of key issues that matter to you. Each book defines the issue, and offers ways of understanding and coping with it.

Real Life Issues aim to demystify the areas that you might find hard to talk about, providing honest facts, practical advice, inspirational quotes and firm reassurance.

Addictions, Stephen Briggs
Confidence and Self-Esteem, Nicki Household
Coping with Life, Jonathan Bradley
Eating Disorders, Heather Warner
Money, Dee Pilgrim
Sex and Relationships, Adele Cherreson
Stress, Rozina Breen

Novels

Inventing Elliot, Graham Gardner, Orion Children's
About a boy who is violently bullied. (For ages 13 upwards.)

Feather Boy, Nicky Singer, Collins

Blubber, Judy Blume, Macmillan Children's Books
(For ages eight to eleven.)

Run, Zan, Run, Catherine MacPhail, Bloomsbury
No one believes that Kate is being bullied – she is accused of attention-seeking by the teacher. (For teenagers.)

Getting Rid of Karenna, Helen Pielichaty, Oxford University Press
A 16-year old starts work at a hairdresser's and finds a school bully working there. (For ages 11–15.)

Forbidden Game, Malorie Blackman, Puffin Books
A boy with sickle cell anaemia rescues the school bully.

The Protectors, Pete Johnson, Puffin Books
Two boys sign up to be anti-bullying counsellors as a way of skiving. They save some children who are being bullied, the power goes to their heads and they become the abusers.

Traitor, Pete Johnson, Corgi Children's
Three children are being bullied by a gang, but one of the children may be in league with the gang.

Four Days Till Friday, Pat Moon, Hodder Children's Books
About friendship, bullying and homosexuality.

Dosh, Robert Swindells, Puffin Books
School protection racket theme. (For ages 13 upwards.)

Cuckoos, Roger Green, Oxford University Press
A boy is being psychologically bullied.

Blue, Sue Mayfield, Hodder Children's Books
Posh Surrey girl moves to Yorkshire school and is befriended by the most popular girl in school only to find that she is not as sweet as she first appeared. (For teenagers.)